Start Now

Grow BIG

Theresa Rose

Theresa Rose

Visit my website at TheresaRose.com for more information or to inquire about volume discounts.

Printed in the United States of America

First Printing: July 2013

Serious Mojo Publications
P.O. Box 385037
Minneapolis, MN 55438

ISBN-13 978-0981886923

Dedication

To Michael and Emma who fill my heart with
BIG love and whose presence in my life make
it the juiciest one imaginable.

Table of Contents

———•••———

Introduction...8

The Trap of Tomorrow 13

   Scarlett Was Wrong 13

   The Sofa Effect......................................14

   The Dream Machine 16

Inviting the Bigger You..........................24

   Growing Big...24

   Smaller Isn't Better...............................27

   Living Freely 31

   Living Fully 47

Introducing The Four Keys to

Transformation......................................58

   The Building Blocks of BIGness 58

The Physical You 61

   The Price of an Empty Tank...................61

   Joy is Your Greatest Motivator...............64

   Permission to Play.................................67

The Mental You 71

   Choice is Your Greatest Asset.................71

   Going from 'I Can't' to 'I Can' 72

The Emotional You 80

   Compassion Is Your Greatest Strategy....80

   Practicing Self-Compassion 81

   Act As-if...84

   Blinded by the Light.............................86

The Spiritual You 91

   Spirit Is Your Greatest Ally 91

Putting It All Together........................100

Resources 105

   Websites 106

   Books 106

   Movies 107

Acknowledgements 108

Book Theresa 109

About the Author 111

"If we did all the things we are capable of, we would literally astound ourselves."

—Thomas Edison

Introduction

—•—

I am just like you. We're all trying to keep 347 balls in the air while still not giving up on our dreams of greater health, pleasure, and financial independence. On one level we are content with our lives as-is. Despite all of the complaining and harrumphing, deep down inside we know how truly blessed we are. We woke up this morning! We have a roof over our heads! We have people who love us! When we get off the frenetic hamster wheel of the perpetual to-do list and take a moment to reflect on our lives, we know that we have it pretty darned good. If you doubt that, it only takes a walk down the street, a click of the remote or a tap on the keyboard to see lots of people who are in tougher shape than we are.

However, that doesn't stop us from wanting more. This book is about growing bigger, both personally and professionally. Whether you want to grow a bigger business, live a bigger life (more joyful and fulfilling), or both, there are four keys to transformation that will help you get there. You will discover that you can transform your physical, mental, emotional and spiritual self by understanding the following guiding principles:

- Joy is your greatest motivator
- Choice is your greatest asset
- Compassion is your greatest strategy
- Spirit is your greatest ally

These lessons are simple, but if you actually put them to work right away instead of just thinking about them, you will literally transform into the You that you've always wanted to be.

Over the last two decades, I have been on a journey of self-discovery and healing that has included a variety of therapies, experiential learning and introspection. In the last few years, my progress has skyrocketed thanks to the emergence of my favorite empowerment tool, the hula hoop. (To get a taste of my passion for All Things Hooping, check out my YouTube channel listed in the Resources section at the back of the book.) My superhero alter-ego is HoopWoman, a rambunctious firecracker who believes that we have the capacity to blow the doors off our potential and embrace our true awesomeness. The hoop is my personal instrument of power, but I am dedicated to helping you realize your own full magnificence with the tools that suit you best. To be clear, this book is not about hooping. It's about expanding our potential beyond our current circumstances.

Despite the differences we have in geography, type of work, family dynamics, pastimes and belief systems, we all have one thing in common: the desire to be happy. We don't want to waste this precious thing called life by spending one more second being depressed and disappointed. We want to live big! I already see you as the powerful, creative beauty that you are, and my job is to provide you with tools that help you see it for yourself. As you transform your inner world, your outer world will begin to expand as well.

'Growing Big' has become a rallying cry that has helped me get through many difficult situations. I constantly ask myself, "Am I big right now? Am I confident, powerful, and fearless? Or have I shrunk down to the small me?" My focus on growing big helps me to become aware of who I am and act more in accordance with my Divine birthright as a Supremely Awesome Chickadee. As a result, my body is healthier than it has ever been, my mind is at peace most of the time, and my business as a professional keynote speaker is thriving. My goal is to help you feel the same way about yourself, day in and day out.

This book is designed to accompany you on your journey to Bigness, and I am very happy to be your guide. Our goal is to free ourselves of the ick that keeps us small and fill ourselves with goodness that will make us huge. Are you ready to go? Let's see what we can discover together!

"I, not events, have the power to make me happy or unhappy today. I can choose which it shall be. Yesterday is dead, tomorrow hasn't arrived yet. I have just one day, today, and I'm going to be happy in it."
— *Groucho Marx*

The Trap of Tomorrow

———◆———

Scarlett Was Wrong

My mother's favorite movie was *Gone with the Wind*. Her favorite character from that movie was, of course, the green-eyed, raven-haired debutante Scarlett O'Hara. Mom loved it when the Civil War diva flounced around declaring to all of her many admirers, "Fiddle dee dee. I'll think about it tomorrow." Ironically, Mom's real-life attitude was diametrically opposed to Scarlett's lackadaisical approach, but she couldn't help but get swept up in the Southern charm of Tara and its occupants. At the end of the movie, Scarlett, overwrought and afraid that her coquettish looks and mesmerizing personality ultimately won't get her what she wants, begs her long-suffering love Rhett Butler not to leave her. In true victim fashion, she pleads, "If you go, where shall I go? What shall I do?!" Rhett, sick and tired of being jerked around by Scarlett ever-so-suavely replies, "Frankly, my dear, I don't give a damn." The sweeping theme music then kicks in with the words "The End" plastered on the screen in ornate script.

In the real world, we don't get end credits. Unlike in many modern movies, things don't get tied up in a pretty bow. Life can be hard. Having a fiddle-dee-dee philosophy will only cause us more pain and agony, causing those around us to eventually stop giving a damn. Like it or not, that message of chronic avoidance got ingrained in the hearts and minds of people everywhere. If something is unpleasant, we can just push it aside, right?

After struggling to find a place of peace and contentment in my own life, I realized that Scarlett was dead wrong. There is no tomorrow. It's a trap. It's a way for us to avoid owning our stuff. Living for tomorrow will Pac-man your life away, minute by minute. When we forego the tough decisions and difficult actions until the fantasy future, we postpone our dreams in favor of the couch.

The Sofa Effect

Fatigue, inertia, habit, and age combined with the cruel effects of gravity are built-in invitations to grow roots on the furniture. Most of our free time is spent in front of a screen, watching reality instead of living it. We all have those big dreams, but we never really seem to get to them. We continue to lie to ourselves by declaring that we'll "start tomorrow". We won't start tomorrow when our tanks are too empty to take the next step. Our moments turn into days, days turn into months, and months turn into a lifetime. "How we spend our days is, of course, how we spend our lives", Annie Dillard once wisely said. Her insight begs the question: How are we spending our lives? Are we balancing our obligations with our aspirations, or are we flooding each day with task after task, never really taking the time to experience the lives we truly want?

We can't afford to wait until tomorrow. We need to start now. We are in a crisis of inactivity and obesity in this world. People are no longer moving, and inactivity is now more deadly than smoking. The energy that we keep trapped in the couch is not available for our creative pursuits. Our life force is going to the E Network instead of our network of friends and family. We are watching "The Real World" instead of living it. The Sofa Effect may be comfortably numbing, but it kidnaps our energy so we no longer have any fuel. Let's decide today to rid ourselves of the allure of the couch and start taking those constructive actions that are in alignment with our highest good! We must begin our journey to bigness with a genuine sense of urgency, because tomorrow is a mystical abyss where our unrealized achievements reside.

The Dream Machine

We all have hopes and desires. We have big dreams. Regardless of the flavor of our wants, we ultimately want to have more, do more and be more. We want to have additional time, money and energy. We want to accomplish more tasks, finish those projects, and express our inherent creativity. We want to be more present with our loved ones, engaged in our communities and grateful for our blessings.

The first step in creating bigness is to identify exactly what it is that we want. We can't go after something if we haven't yet defined it. Let's take some time together now to create a dream machine. Don't worry about how you are going to get there; just think about what you want. Your job is not to figure it all out, but rather to determine what you want to have. So, let's open some doors and bust through some ceilings to see what kind of lives we can create, shall we? What do we want out of life? It's time to dust off our unspoken hopes and put a plan in place to get there. Once we identify what our dreams are, the four keys to transformation will be our guideposts to make them a reality.

Exercise

What is your dream? Be specific as possible and use extra paper if you need to. Think about what you want to accomplish in terms of your health, relationships, career, finances, travel, recreation, and charity.

_____

_____

_____

_____

_____

_____

_____

_____

_____

_____

_____

If you could create the perfect life, what would it be?

_____

_____

_____

_____

_____

_____

_____

_____

_____

_____

_____

How will realizing your dream affect you physically?

_____

_____

_____

_____

How will realizing your dream affect you mentally?

_____

_____

_____

_____

How will realizing your dream affect you emotionally?

_____

_____

_____

_____

_____

_____

How will realizing your dream affect you spiritually?

_____

_____

_____

_____

_____

Is that dream really yours or someone else's? If it is someone else's, whose is it and why have you convinced yourself that you need to do it?

_____

_____

_____

_____

_____

Do you want your dream badly enough to endure the difficult challenges you'll face along the way, and what will you do to get through the rough spots?

_____

_____

_____

_____

_____

After defining what it is that you want, now let's look at how you are spending your most valuable resource -- your time -- in pursuit of that dream.

Exercise

What activities make up a typical day for you? Write down everything that you do from the moment you wake up in the morning until the moment you put your head on the pillow at the end of the day. Make a checkmark in the 'O' column next to those activities that are done for others, an 'S' next to those things that are done for you, an 'E' next to those items that provide an escape, e.g. watching TV, surfing the Internet, etc. and a 'D' next to those items that are in support of your dreams.

No.	Task	O	S	E	D
1.					
2.					
3.					
4.					
5.					
6.					
7.					
8.					
9.					
10.					
11.					
12.					
13.					
14.					
15.					
16.					
17.					
18.					
19.					
20.					

What does this exercise tell you about your values and priorities?

_____

_____

_____

_____

_____

What specific changes could you make to better align your activities with your values?

_____

_____

_____

_____

_____

Power Statement

I will not coast through life, hoping that tomorrow will be better. I will take action now in support of my dreams.

"The greater danger for most of us lies not in setting our aim too high and falling short, but in setting our aim too low, and achieving our mark."
—Michaelangelo

Inviting the Bigger You

Growing Big

Over the last twenty years I have spent countless hours and thousands of dollars on healing therapies, self-help books, enrichment classes, business coaching sessions, empowerment workshops and spiritual retreats. I have focused on everything from freeing my Inner Child to clearing my chakras. Each path promised the holy grail of balance, success and happiness while offering a specific recipe for how to attain it. After two decades of trying everything under the sun to make more sense out of this experience called life, I realize that everything points to one simple yet mysterious solution: GROWING BIG.

Growing big means embodying your fullest potential. It's about yummy living. It's walking through each day with your head held high and your heart wide open. It's about getting on the stage of life and acting as if there is a live audience and not just a mere dress rehearsal. It's going after what you want despite the fear that is present within you. If you are in a really bad place in your life, growing big may not necessarily mean lighting the world on fire, but it may mean having a better day today than you had yesterday. Maybe it means that you get out of bed a little earlier than usual. No matter where you are on the spectrum of joy, well-being and abundance, you can always take another step toward a bigger, better future.

When we grow big, our bodies get healthier and our wallets get fatter. Our relationships flourish and our communities strengthen. We grow into the powerful people we are destined to be, not just robots trudging through each day. Growing big will make our time on earth juicy and delicious.

Exercise

What does the Big You look like?

_____

_____

_____

_____

_____

How does the Big You spend her days?

_____

_____

_____

_____

_____

What relationships does she have?

_____

_____

_____

_____

_____

Describe the aspects of the Big You that you would like to have the most.

_____

_____

_____

_____

Smaller Isn't Better

We are taught from a very early age that small is good. As a lifelong overeater, I have been trying to get smaller my entire life. My childhood was filled with hurtful nicknames hurled at me from schoolyard bullies, causing me to wear bulky clothing to hide my shapeless body. I had a persistent desire to fill my gullet with food, anesthetizing the pain of a seemingly unhealable wound in my soul. My dreams were filled with images of me in a smaller, firmer body where others responded positively to the tinier me. It was only when I reached my 42nd year on the planet that I realized I should be focusing on getting bigger, not smaller.

In my experience, there are many more small people than big people out there. It's like living in Oz without the lollipops and yellow brick road. In a country whose inhabitants are growing wider by the minute, paradoxically we are also shrinking energetically. Through the manipulation of the media and other cultural culprits, we are convinced that who we are is simply not good enough. Somehow we are lacking. We keep telling ourselves that we are not living the lives we would like to be living, and we repeat this lie over and over as if we are powerless to do anything about it. Because we keep telling ourselves this untruth, it eventually becomes our reality. Instead of the boy who cried wolf, we are the girls and boys who cried small. We cried it long enough and loud enough and, lo and behold, smallness came to us.

Small people are afraid, self-conscious and negative. They don't have very much life force within them, and the little they have is directed toward surviving rather than thriving. Smallness is the unconscious incorporation of 'not-enough'-ness. It keeps us terrified of what other people think. It places our reality light years away from our potential.

In Smallville, we live in an "If only" world of long-forgotten dreams. Our tanks are empty, and we are coasting through life rather than blazing through it. Small people are living 'less-than' and they are not happy about it. Because they are unhappy about it, they want you to be unhappy too. They have no goals, no dreams, and no positive impact on the community. Every day is filled with chronic complaining, missed opportunities, and dashed expectations. In short, small people see the world through poop-colored glasses!

Exercise

In what ways are you currently living smaller than you would like?

_____

_____

_____

_____

_____

Who are the small people in your life?

_____

_____

_____

_____

_____

What behaviors and attitudes make them small?

_____

_____

_____

_____

_____

How do you feel when you spend time with them?

_____

_____

_____

Why do you spend time with them?

_____

_____

_____

_____

_____

Is there a way you can minimize your exposure to them or make the interactions more pleasant?

_____

_____

_____

_____

_____

We know our time here is temporary. It's the nature of the gig, and we signed up for it. We will be gone one day, as will every single person we love. Yet, we let silly stuff get in the way of our happiness. Since the collective consciousness of smallness is powerful and pervasive, we have a natural tendency to fall into that trap. You are not meant to live a life of mediocrity! You are meant to suck every last drop of juice out of your brief time here on earth. Living freely and living fully are two components of growing big.

Living Freely

Freedom. It's one of the cornerstones of our culture, and maintaining it is something for which many brave warriors have given their lives. Thanks to them, we are free...but only to a certain extent. We are held prisoner by the self-induced emotional captors of shame, fear, and victimhood.

Shame

"I just feel compelled to continue to be transparent. It just really levels the playing field and eradicates the shame that I have, or that one might have, about being human. So I'm going to just keep going."
—Alanis Morrissette

Shame is that sniveling, mean-spirited little voice that dances around our grey matter and tells us we're not good enough, pretty enough, rich enough, successful enough, tall enough, young enough, thin enough, enlightened enough and/or fashionable enough. We're just not...enough. Shame is a virus that got installed early on in our mental CPUs that keeps perpetuating itself. Hollywood has us believing that we all should be without flaws. When I consider that the freakishly perfect Jennifer Aniston and I are the same age, I sometimes succumb to that media nonsense and want to hurl myself out the window. The truth of the matter is that most normal, female homo sapiens over forty years of age have skin-wings, not sculpted art for arms. (Michelle Obama must also be from the same planetary system as Ms. Aniston. Et tu, FLOTUS?)

I want to be free of that sickening, quiet little feeling that I am less-than because I am not the perfect cardboard cutout of what a woman should be. Modern technological "advances" coupled with Photoshop finagling have made it possible to mask the natural aging process. We see more and more images of these freaks-of-nature women who make it look like it's normal to have a cellulite-free figure, beach balls for boobs, a stomach you could bounce quarters on, a heart-shaped butt, a sun-kissed tan all year around, attractive feet sporting a fresh pedicure in 5-inch stilettos, triple highlighted and lowlighted locks that flow like freshly-spun silk, and a set of pearly whites that require sunglasses to view.

This is what women have to live with, and it's high time we stop the madness. We don't need to look like porn stars. We don't have to go under the knife to be beautiful. We don't need to compare ourselves to an unreasonable, not-of-this-earth version of "the perfect woman". Men get bald, men get fat, and men get wrinkles. Nobody seems to be causing a ruckus about that. Why are women expected to have every last flaw removed in order to be noticed and appreciated?!

Enough is enough. I will never be able to compete with perfection, so I am taking myself out of the contest entirely. My appearance needs to satisfy only one person: me! If I think I rock, then I rock. I don't give a rat's silicone-implanted butt if I am seen as an over-the-hill, overweight wrinkle-bag who shouldn't be wearing what I'm wearing. That's just too darned bad if others can't recognize my awesomeness.

Let's be free of the belief that we are less-than. We have Spirit inside of us! It is the most powerful force in the Universe! Let's rid ourselves of shame and take delight in the beauty of our bodies as the Creator created them.

Exercise

What parts of you cause you to feel shame?

_____
_____
_____
_____

To whom are you comparing yourself?

_____
_____
_____
_____

Who installed that belief in you?

_____
_____
_____
_____

How can you reframe your so-called flaws and see them as flairs?

_____
_____
_____
_____

Fear

*"We gain strength, and courage, and confidence by each experience in which we really stop to look fear in the face… we must do that which we think we cannot." —**Eleanor Roosevelt***

Fear isn't real. It's a mental illusion we have concocted to pre-pave the nastiest possible outcome. We let this Fallacy From Hell take over our mental body and paralyze us from taking action. It is a demon. Fear bubbles appear so quickly, easily and voluminously. There are reality TV shows dedicated to preying on people's deepest, darkest fears. How twisted is it that observing someone in the throes of a panic attack constitutes entertainment?

I don't perceive fear as something we can just carve out and put aside. It's not an emotional appendix that can be easily removed with some anesthesia and a sharp knife. Instead, the energy of fear is interwoven within us. It permeates us in the stories we tell, memories we hold, and wounds we bear. It convinces us not to trust or believe and invites us to worry that what comes next will have the worst possible outcome.

I bet if you and I sat down for a coffee or adult beverage and asked each other, "what are you afraid of?", a whole boat-load of dialogue would ensue. What have I been afraid of? The short answer is nearly everything. Here are some oldies but moldies that have haunted me:

- Fear of failure
- Fear of success
- Fear of loneliness
- Fear of something bad happening to a member of my family
- Fear of running out of money
- Fear of getting sick and dying
- Fear of being in a horrible, disfiguring accident
- Fear of calling too much attention to myself
- Fear of people physically threatening me or my family because they don't approve of what I do/say/write/think/am
- Fear of criticism
- Fear of fear

For me, fear is like cement. It holds me firmly in place, not allowing me to move forward. It keeps me in an illusory state of comfort and safety, but in reality it is killing me. I hate knowing that I am not acting on something simply because I am scared witless of doing it. When my mom was a Mary Kay Senior Sales Director, her standard closing line when speaking with a potential recruit was, "Other than fear, is there any reason why you wouldn't want to begin your training program today?" I can thank her for teaching me at such an early age how fear plays a role in our decision-making process.

When we have a life that isn't dominated by fear and approach new opportunities with a resounding "YES, great things are going to happen!", then our whole world changes. Anodea Judith, one of my teachers, often exclaims, "Thank you, thank you, thank you! I deserve this. Send me more!" This phrase imprints YES into our energy and puts us in the powerful vibration of gratitude. Mary Morissey describes gratitude as "the feeling tone of the state of abundance." By saying yes more than we say no, we turn feardom into freedom.

Fear is the perfume of the Small Me. The Small Me covers herself in it, reeks of it, and pushes people away because of it. It's a crusty old bottle of *Charlie* for the soul. Frankly, I'd rather wear *Chanel No. 5*, thank you very much. Let's pour that foul stench of fear down the drain for good. We can be free of the straightjacket of wussiness once and for all. There is nothing out there that is out to get us. We are supported, and we won't fail. It's time to take the training wheels off and ride around the neighborhood with the wind in our hair.

Exercise

What are your fears?

_____
_____
_____
_____

From where or from whom did they originate?

_____
_____
_____
_____

What does it feel like when you allow those fears to drive your actions?

_____
_____
_____
_____

How realistic is it that those fears will actually come to fruition?

_____
_____
_____
_____

Instead of focusing on your fears, for what can you be grateful?

_____

_____

_____

_____

Victimhood

"If it's never our fault, we can't take responsibility for it. If we can't take responsibility for it, we'll always be its victim."
— **Richard Bach**

Victimhood is a dastardly foe, telling us that something or somebody else is responsible for our happiness. It is the insidious voice inside of us that says that we aren't in charge. It is the voice that tells us how friggin' hard everything is. It is the voice that tells us there isn't anything we can do about the negative stuff that happens in our lives.

It's important to note that victimhood is not the same as feeling pain. Everyone has painful experiences. If you made a laundry list of all of the crappy things that have transpired in your lifetime, I bet you would be writing for a long time. I could probably fill a narrow-ruled, 3-subject binder before even getting to high school. Most of us have histories that could easily be made into a a Lifetime Movie of the Week starring Melissa Gilbert. I am not saying that you have to ignore those things that were difficult or pretend they didn't exist. I am certainly not saying that you shouldn't fully express your emotions, and I would never recommend numbing out. However, victimhood comes into play when you allow those crappy things that have happened keep you afraid, angry, depressed and stuck in the past.

The word 'victim' is often used as a way for us to name our wounds. We take stuff that has happened to us and put them in buckets with labels on them. When something really tragic befalls us, we often say that we are a victim of it. We say, "I am a car accident victim", "I am a sexual abuse victim", or "I am a victim of corporate layoffs." Some small people who have experienced great pain have permanently attached themselves to the word victim. They've interwoven with that word so much that 'victim' is them and they are victims. When victimhood becomes a core component of our personality, depression and stress are present every day. Really painful, tragic experiences can happen to us in our lives that split our hearts wide open, but it doesn't have to make us victims.

Victims are people who have forgotten that they are connected to a Higher Source. Because they perceive them—

selves as powerless, they have simply given their joy away. They have checked out, and so they fall back on blame. "It's your fault that this bad thing happened" and "why can't I have the life I want?" They get themselves all worked up about something they think they had nothing to do with. They may not be responsible for the negative thing that took place initially, but they sure as heck own their reaction to it.

One of the most profound changes you can make to break free from victimhood is to change your language. The two favorite words a victim uses are "have to". A simple reframing from "have to" to "get to" will change your life. I am so aware of the negative power that the phrase "have to" evokes in me and the lives of those around me. "I have to do this, I have to do that!" My daughter Emma is a ball of energy right up until I say, "Emma, you have to clean your room." Immediately upon hearing this, all of her energy deflates like a runaway balloon and she begins the laborious process of begging, cajoling and otherwise weaseling her way out of doing it. (I'm convinced that they are teaching Advanced Negotiation Skills starting at the elementary school level.) Oftentimes, she'll do a sloppy job of it because she didn't want to do the exercise, she *had* to do it. Sadly, the habit I notice in my daughter is much like my own. I will, on the surface, seem like a very busy, task-oriented, responsible adult, but inside when I tell myself that I have to do something -- laundry, bills, work, grocery shop, work out, or lose weight -- and bring the 'have to' energy along with it, I will act just like my daughter cleaning her room. Sometimes I have an adult version of a temper tantrum, silently screaming, "No, I don't want to! Why do I have to do that? I don't wanna!"

Consider how often we hear, "I have to go to work." In actuality, no one has to go to work. Nobody is putting a gun to our heads to force us to do our in-home jobs or drive to our places of employment every weekday. If we decide not to go to work, we will experience whatever happens as a result. (Losing the job is one obvious example.) We make a choice. We choose to have the opportunity to earn money in exchange for our energy, and as a result, we get to enjoy the lifestyles we have chosen. In fact, we GET to go to work. Many people in the world would love to have our jobs, regardless of how horrible we may think they are. The money we earn goes towards things we appreciate, like food, shelter, clothing and recreation. It's an exchange; one to which we all willingly agreed. This example holds true for every other area in our lives, including our bodies, relationships and communities.

When we start releasing some of that small, constricted, compressed, solid energy of "No, I can't; I'm afraid; it's all his fault; I have to", our bodies start to open up and more of who we really are, our Higher Selves, can enter in. That Higher

Self tells us that everything is happening exactly as it should. Even if an event was very painful, we can still recognize that it contained a precious gift. It taught us something. It showed us something. It prompted us to feel. Walking in the world with a "get to" attitude makes us bigger.

Victimhood makes us complain about every little thing: "I can't believe how bad the traffic is today!", "I don't have time to do this!", "My boss is an idiot!", "Why can't my spouse/child/co-worker do what I ask?"

On any given day I might forget that I own my happiness and slide into an unconscious funk. Here is but a small list of "Have-to's" that I have uttered recently:

- Oh man, I have to go to work.
- I have to go to the grocery store. Again.
- I have to do the blasted laundry.
- Why do I have to wash the dishes every single time?[1]
- I have to answer all of these emails and return calls.
- I have to clean the house. Again.
- Jeez, I have to write that proposal before the end of the day!
- I have to pay the #@%* bills.
- Aargh! I have to get to the airport!
- I have to fold my husband's skivvies. Again.
- Oh great. I have to get the car serviced.

---

1. My husband staunchly disagrees with this assessment, but he is, as always, delusional as regards the divvying up of domestic responsibilities.

- I'm running late and have to get Emma to karate class!

What a burden! It's downright depressing.

Then I remind myself that I don't have to do any of it. I choose to do them. I can always decide that I want to have a life as a slovenly, homeless, lonely slug. That is a choice on my part. So, instead of 'have to', I try to remind myself that I not only *choose* to do those things, I *get* to do them. Notice the different energy of the reframed reality:

- I get to go to work. (Yay, I have a job!)
- I get to go to the grocery store. (Yay, we can buy food instead of having to grow it all ourselves!)
- I get to do laundry. (Yay, I don't have to wear soiled, stinky clothes!)
- I get to wash the dishes. (Yay, we are able to make delicious meals at home that are healthier and more affordable than going out to eat.)
- I get to answer a bunch of emails and return calls. (Yay, there are people that want to work with me!)
- I get to clean the house. (Yay, there's a house to clean!)
- I get to write a proposal. (Yay, someone wants to hire me!)
- I get to fold my husband's skivvies. (Yay, I have a husband who I love and loves me! Bonus: He wears underwear!)

- I get to pay the bills. (Yay, we are able to have electricity, phone service, heat, and water!)
- I get to go the airport. (Yay, I don't have to drive three days to get to Florida!)
- I get to have my car serviced. (Yay, I have a car that gets me from point A to point B instead of having to walk or take the bus!)
- I get to take my daughter to karate class. (Yay, Emma is fortunate enough to take advantage of this wonderful practice! Or even better, Yay, Emma is in my life!)

I am the first to admit that this is not easy. The habit is so firmly entrenched in most of us that it pops out without us even noticing. However, I am striving to free myself from the lie that I am not the owner of my emotions. No matter what happens to us, no one is responsible for how we react but us. If we want to be in a snit-fit because of the unconscious actions of others, it's our fault, not theirs. Let's not allow any yahoo to occupy our heads rent-free.

Exercise

What is your list of "Have-to's"?

_____

_____

_____

_____

_____

_____

_____

_____

_____

_____

Rewrite them as "Get-to's" so you can establish a healthier relationship with your daily activities.

_____

_____

_____

_____

_____

_____

_____

_____

_____

_____

Living Fully

Once you free yourself of all that ishy stuff, you can let your Divine energy shine through! Your spirit is made up of three things: Joy, Love, and Power. You deserve to have it all.

Joy

"Joy is what happens to us when we allow ourselves to recognize how good things really are." — **Marianne Williamson**

When you start getting rid of all that is keeping you small, resentful, and depressed, you make room for joy. You will feel joy because you are experiencing life fully and embracing new adventures! You share your life with others. Beauty surrounds you. Nature is bountiful. Every day contains magic.

There is a universal law that has been in place from the time of the first human on the planet until this very moment. This law is applicable to every single person who has ever drawn a breath: *we all want to experience joy in one form or another*.

No two people have the same goals, yet all goals are just offshoots of that same universal desire for joy. The caveman may have wanted to ensure that he killed a wildebeest before sundown so he and his family could feel good by surviving another day. Shakespeare wrote a kajillion plays because it made him feel good to express himself creatively and have people perform his works for appreciative audiences. Warriors have gone to war because they believe that winning the battle will provide themselves, their loved ones, and their country with better, more joyful lives. Those nutty Iron Man competitors run, swim and bike like maniacs because accomplishing that physically exhaustive race makes them feel good (although I can't for the life of me understand why).

All of your dreams and goals boil down to their ability to elicit joy for you. Whether your goal is to get a husband (or get rid of the husband), get a better job, improve your home, gain weight, lose weight, climb Mount Everest, or meet Johnny Depp, you believe that attaining those things will bring you joy.

When we are full of joy, we approach life like a carnival instead of an IRS tax audit. Life is just too darned short to be depressed or angry all of the time.

Exercise

What brings you joy?

_____

_____

_____

_____

Who brings you joy?

_____

_____

_____

_____

How often do you experience joy?

_____

_____

_____

_____

Is there anything that makes you feel you do not deserve joy?

_____

_____

_____

_____

Love

"Love yourself first and everything else falls into line. You really have to love yourself to get anything done in this world."
— *Lucille Ball*

Everybody wants to love and be loved in return. Everybody craves connection with another. A pulsating heart wants to find another so it can connect to its vibration, to its energy. Our lives deserve to be filled with lots of love from the community, those closest to us, our partners, and most importantly, ourselves. If we can't truly love ourselves, then our attempts at giving love to others are likely to falter.

That muscle in the center of our chest does more than keep blood pumping in our meat suits. It is a receptacle for love. When it is full, we are full. When it is lacking, we are lacking. Whether it is for your spouse, your child or your adorable King Charles spaniel, the love that emanates from this energy cavity is what makes life worth living. However, when we are small, the space allotted for love gets small too.

Smallness brings about emotions contrary to love — things like jealousy, anger, and self-loathing. Small people ask themselves, "Why would this person fall in love with me? What is there to love? S/he will undoubtedly find someone more lovable in the near future, and I'll be left all alone."

Boy, doesn't THAT sound attractive? Smallness is about as alluring as wearing a rotting rhino carcass in place of a feather boa.

When we grow big, we fundamentally become more attractive to others, both romantically and energetically. I know that from my own experience, I can see the difference in how strangers relate to me when I am big versus small. The greatest test environment is a busy airport. When I am feeling big, I stand a little taller, I walk with greater confidence, and there is a smile on my face and a sashay in my hips. The TSA dudes are friendlier, the other passengers take a peek my way a bit more often, and sometimes I even get upgraded. However, when I am small, it's like I am wearing a sign on my chest that says, "Life Sucks and So Do I." Whether they are conscious of it or not, people gravitate toward big people and shy away from the wee ones.

Exercise

Who do you love?

_____
_____
_____
_____

What do you love?

_____
_____
_____
_____

In what ways do you express your love to others?

_____
_____
_____
_____

What actions can you take today in support of that which you love?

_____
_____
_____
_____

<u>Power</u>

"The most common way people give up their power is by thinking they don't have any." — *Alice Walker*

The word 'power' has been hijacked. We have been trained to believe that power is bad. Power is what "the man" uses to keep the rest of us down. Power is for those who have no heart. Power is wielded like a sword. However, just as the 220 volt outlet doesn't have an evil agenda to kill you, so too power remains neutral. It can be tremendously productive or tremendously destructive, depending on the intention of the person wielding it. The solar panels on your roof aren't part of the Axis of Evil. They are merely conductors of energy. You are a conductor of energy. What you do with power is up to you. The more energy or power you have, the more you can do with it, either for good or evil.

Let's say you want to do good with your power. If you wake up in the morning with a spring in your step that propels your day forward, you will get more accomplished than if you drag your butt around like you have just gotten a double epidural. You have more fuel, more fire, more zest to accomplish big things. Let's shine like the lighthouse that guides sailors safely home instead of the soft glow of a nightlight that illuminates the way to the bathroom. Let's make a difference by utilizing our power to its fullest, most glorious extent.

Imagine what we could accomplish in our lives if we consistently told ourselves this reality instead:

We are:

- Perfectly content with our financial health while being open to more abundance
- Perfectly content with our bodies while being open to having greater health and vitality
- Perfectly content with our jobs while being open to greater professional fulfillment
- Perfectly content with our spirituality while being open to deepening our connection
- Perfectly content with our relationships while being open to more love

I don't know about you, but when I think about those realities, my first reaction is a sigh of relief and a smile on my face. Instead of wasting precious energy continuing to perpetuate the lie of limitation, we can refocus our energies on accomplishing the things we want to do! Personally, I would spend more of my time on writing books, performing, and doing fun stuff with my family instead of surfing Facebook, reading InTouch magazine, or tuning into the latest Reality TV trash-du-jour. Imagine what the world would look like if everyone's potential matched their reality? What amazing things would take place and be created?

Exercise

What would you accomplish if you had more power?

_____

_____

_____

_____

What contributions would you make to your local and global communities?

_____

_____

_____

_____

What are your feelings about becoming a more powerful individual?

_____

_____

_____

_____

Are there any negative thoughts or perceptions you have about power, and if so, how can you reframe them to something entirely positive?

_____

_____

Power Statement

I am ready to accept my bigness
and expand into my fullest potential.

"Transformation literally means going beyond your form." —**Wayne Dyer**

Introducing The Four Keys to Transformation

———◆◆———

The Building Blocks of BIGness

Transformation is a process, not something that takes place at a discreet point in time. As we accept the challenge to start now and grow big, we need to recognize the building blocks that will help us get there. Transformation takes place in every part of us that contributes to our footprint in the world: our physical, mental, emotional and spiritual selves. By caring for and feeding all four of these parts of you on an ongoing basis, you will find yourself moving from a small pond to an expansive ocean. Through a combination of power, presence and play, you will maximize your energetic output and start co-creating the life you are meant to live.

When we consciously and consistently nurture these four fundamental aspects of ourselves, our worlds begin to open up in ways in which we never would have dreamed. Possibility becomes probability. Probability becomes inevitability. Maybe becomes yes.

Power Statement

———

I am creating the life I want by transforming myself physically, mentally, emotionally and spiritually.

The Physical You

The Price of an Empty Tank

Whether it's the creation of a healthier body, a better relationship, or a thriving business, success is dependent upon the fuel that propels it. This fuel is our mojo, that fire that burns within us, our Life Force Energy. Its presence can make life exhilarating, and its absence can make life exhausting.

When our tanks are full, we can consciously create our days exactly as we wish them to unfold. We wake up in the morning feeling great, jump out of bed with a spring in our step, do our morning process, get dressed in well-fitting, clean clothes that make us feel comfortable, enjoy a delicious, healthy breakfast, start our workday with grace and ease, attend to all of the daily tasks, and essentially see the day flow as we want it. Decisions are being made quickly and efficiently, and happy people surround us. We have ample time to tackle all of the activities on our plates. We return home to make a wonderful, healthy meal that we joyfully prepare with our families and have great dinner table conversations. Afterwards we even have some extra fuel left to move our bodies, spend quiet time in meditation or work on that special writing, crafting or other creative project we want to complete. By the end of the night, we climb into bed happily knowing that we sucked every last drop out of every moment of the day. Mission accomplished.

How often do we have days like these? Sadly, our days are often spent like this instead...

6:00am. The alarm goes off. You're angry. You are shocked that it could already be six o'clock since it feels like you just laid your head down on the pillow a few minutes ago. You hit the snooze bar in an attempt to steal 9, 18 or 27 more minutes of sleep before you have to get to work. Your first conscious thought is that you feel like you might be coming down with something. You crunch, creak and crackle out of bed, stubbing your toe on your way to the bathroom. As you brush your teeth, you think, "Yep, I definitely feel like I am coming down with something." You eek out a tiny cough on your way to the closet zone. As you suspected, you can't find anything decent to wear because the laundry hasn't been done. Since you are already running late, you settle for an old black sweater that you've worn at least a hundred times before. You snarf down a bowl of Chocolate Flavored Honey Puffs while finishing your morning routine. On your way to work, you realize that you are almost out of gas and will need to fill up before you get on the highway that you *know* will have a traffic jam at that hour. (Which in fact, it does.) By the time you get to work, you are already annoyed and exhausted, waiting for that third cup of coffee to kick in. You are overwhelmed by your workload with towers of paper on your desk and dozens of emails choking your Inbox. You feel like you are running an hour behind all day long, not seemingly able to catch up. Finally, finally, finally the end of the work day mercifully arrives, and you can't wait to get out of there. On the way home you realize that you don't have anything for dinner and, because no one else will plan anything, you are going to have to stop and buy a bag of food-like substances at your neighborhood fast food establishment. By the time you get home, unwrap the dinner, inhale it, and throw its remnants away, you are so exhausted that all you have the energy to do is bust open the box of wine, break out a bag of Funyuns and boob out to the latest episode of the *American Hoarding Housewives of the Dancing Kardashians*. By the end of the evening, you barely have enough steam to turn off the clicker and collapse into bed. Another day older, another day wasted.

Why do we have so many more of the latter days than

the former? Why can't we seem to get into the groove? Why is every day so hard?

We know what we want, but we don't have the motivation to go after it. Joyful movement will help us get started on our journey.

Joy is Your Greatest Motivator

"Just play. Have fun. Enjoy the game." —**Michael Jordan**

When I clocked in at nearly 200 pounds on my statuesque 5'3" frame, I did not know about the power of joyful movement. Back then, I operated as one big head, completely divorced from what might be going on south of the collarbone. I hated exercise and exerted only enough physical energy to keep upright. Even the word 'exercise' gives me the heebee-jeebees! It's too close to the word 'exorcise', which conjures up images of a she-demon spinning her head in a full 360 while vomiting green goo, and that's just me on the elliptical after 30 minutes. I hate it! Most days I harrumphed from one locale to another, pining for the horizontal goodness of my queen size bed every night. Except for the occasional embarrassing, champagne-fueled, interpretive dance of "Brick House" at a distant relative's wedding, I just didn't like to move.

That is, until the hoop came into my life.

The arrival of the hoop started my love affair with joyful movement. Hooping helped me to shed more than fifty pounds, and more importantly, it helped me to keep it off. Losing weight isn't the hard part. It's finding it again that presents the challenge! I've lost thousands of pounds in my life, but they always seem to find their way back to me. That was, until I met the hoop. It is proven to burn calories, strengthen your core, and improve flexibility, grace and balance. But, let's be honest. There are tons of gadgets, gym equipment and group classes that could have gotten me there years ago. What is the difference? Hooping makes me happy.

The hoop is my spiraling sacred container where I discover more of who I really am. Yes, hooping is a workout. It is also a natural antidepressant, a profound meditation, an empowerment workshop, a brainstorming session, a personal coaching appointment, and a dance party all rolled into one beautiful, sparkly circle. The joy contained in this hoop kept me going, even when the allure of the couch called to me. The joy grew me. HoopLove was instrumental in creating the Bigger Me. When we give more conscious attention to our bodies, we discover that our greatest motivator in the process of creation is JOY. Remember, my joyful movement of choice is the hoop; yours may be something totally different. It doesn't matter what you do to move, as long as you do it from a place of satisfaction.

Joy drives every single one of our actions, because despite all of our excuses and proclamations, we don't ever do anything we don't really want to do. If we really want to do something, we create space for it and follow through. I *will* find the time to watch every single movie awards show with corresponding red carpet pre-show coverage. I *will* find the money to get my hair done by Bob, the only man other than my husband that I would follow anywhere. I *will* find the energy to help out a cause or worthy organization that stirs my soul. When we change our attitude towards movement from being that of a chore to being one of privilege, then we make time for it. We schedule play dates for our children; why can't we do it for ourselves? ("HoopJam: Wednesdays at 7:00pm!")

Permission to Play

"Women in particular need to keep an eye on their physical and mental health, because if we're scurrying to and from appointments and errands, we don't have a lot of time to take care of ourselves. We need to do a better job of putting ourselves higher on our own 'to do' list." — **Michelle Obama**

The healthier and stronger our bodies are, the more physical energy we will possess. The more energy we possess, the more we can accomplish. Joy waters the seeds of our desires by giving us the fuel we need to keep going, even when it's challenging. My movement of choice is the hula hoop, but for you it might be a Zumba class, a round of golf, a tennis match, or even a spirited game of naked Twister! Identify some fun ways you can increase your activity every single day -- do a little yoga before bedtime, take one more walk with your four-legged loved one, find your inner dancing queen with a rousing session of car-dancing, or dust off those bikes in the garage and take a ride around the neighborhood. After the New Year's resolutions have worn off, the motivation to keep moving comes from joy. Joy is the catalyst that takes us from the couch to the playground. You don't need to exercise, but you absolutely have permission to play.

Exercise

What do you love do do?

_____

_____

_____

_____

How do you love to play?

_____

_____

_____

_____

How do you move through life?

_____

_____

_____

_____

What fun things can you do to move your body more?

_____

_____

_____

_____

Power Statement

My body is strong, vibrant, healthy
and supportive of all that
I want to accomplish.

"You have a choice. Live or die. Every breath is a choice. Every minute is a choice. To be or not to be."
— **Chuck Palahniuk**

The Mental You

Choice is Your Greatest Asset

When we give more conscious attention to our thoughts, we discover that our greatest asset in the process of creation is CHOICE. Our thoughts are merely precursors to the choices we make. If we continue to choose a mindset of limitation and lack, we will not see the opportunities presenting themselves to us, or they won't present themselves at all. We have a choice in every single moment. We choose to believe whether we can or cannot accomplish something. We choose if our dreams are possible or impossible. We choose whether we are deserving of happiness or not. When we no longer make choices from a place of victimhood but instead from a place of power, the landscape of our lives begins to expand.

A critical choice we can make towards the attainment of our dreams is to silence our Inner Victim. The victim inside tells us that life is so hard, that someone or something else is responsible for our happiness, and that there isn't anything we can do about it. When we convince ourselves that we have to do something as opposed to choosing to do something -- or better yet, *getting* to do something -- we continue to stay in a victim mentality. That mentality convinces us that our options are limited; that we have no choices. When we feed the program of victimhood and lack of choice, our opportunities dry up because we don't even see them. The landscape of possibility shrinks.

Going from 'I Can't' to 'I Can'

When we accept that our thoughts are things we can control through conscious choice, we can choose a new reality moment after moment after moment. Instead of suffering through a have-to reality, we can create a get-to reality. Every summer, I get to hoopdance outdoors in my beautiful hometown of Minneapolis. There's nothing like it! The sun is shining, the birds are singing, and the hoops are flying. Life is good. My favorite place in the world to hoop is on the gorgeous banks of Lake Harriet. As you can imagine, I elicit a few double-takes when I bust some moves by the lake. It's not every day you see a 40-something suburban mom dance with a glittery hoop. Oftentimes people will come up to me and say "that looks like a lot of fun!", "I bet it's great exercise", or "I used to do that as a kid!" Sometimes people will just have a terrified look on their faces and utter, "you are very, very brave". But, there is one comment that I hear most frequently, whether I am hooping by Lake Harriet, the Gulf of Mexico, the Pacific Ocean or all points in between. I hear the same four, sad words: "I can't do that." The vast majority of people who strike up a hoop conversation with me have said those four words. Guess what? There was a time when I couldn't do these things either! When I started I couldn't keep the hoop from falling to the ground every few seconds. Things change. We learn. We practice. We grow. There is a moment for all of us when we go from 'I can't' to 'I can'. Yet, we continue to reinforce the limiting mental belief that we can't do something just because we haven't done it yet.

Let me tell you a story about a woman named Shirley. I met Shirley in a hotel bar in Des Moines. As the bartender with a scowly face and imposing figure, Surly Shirley definitely made an impression. I was on my way to the sundeck with my trusty hoop in hand when Shirley stopped me.

"What is that? Is that a hula hoop?"

"Yep, it sure is."

"Do you know how to use it?"

"Yep, I'm a speaker and I use it in my speaking pres..."

"Show me."

"What, here?"

"Yeah."

The cramped space filled with four-tops and the omnipresent faux ferns did not provide an optimal hooping environment. However, never one to shy away from an opportunity to share the power of the hoop, of course I took her up on it. I did a few simple waist hooping rotations and a few over-the-head lifts for good measure.

"I can't do that."

I told Shirley what I tell every single person who tells me those four words:

"Sure you can. You just didn't have the right hoop."

Shirley was not convinced.

"Why don't you try my hoop and see for yourself?"

As soon as I offered her the chance to try it, Shirley immediately jumped out from behind the bar, grabbed the hoop from my hands, put it over her head, and got into position. With her scowl still firmly emblazoned on her face, Shirley said,

"Oh, all right. I'll try it just so you can feel better about yourself."

I gave Shirley a quick Hooping 101 lesson: give it a good toss, keep it parallel to the ground, place one foot in front of the other, and move your hips back and forth. In no time, Shirley was swinging her booty like she was at Studio 54 jamming with Gloria Gaynor. Her frown immediately disappeared and was replaced with a gorgeous, toothy grin. After a few minutes the hoop dropped, as all hoops eventually do. Shirley begrudgingly returned the hoop to me and cheered, "You just added ten years to my life!"

Just because we haven't done something in the past doesn't mean we can't do it now *if* we have the right tools, instruction, support and environment. When our conversation began, Shirley believed that she was unable to hoop. However, she proved to herself and everyone else in the bar that with the right hoop, she could be successful.

Before Shirley and I said goodbye, I left her with these final thoughts:

"You never thought you could hula hoop before today. You said, 'I can't do that.' A few minutes ago, in your bar, you proved that you could. Do me a favor, Shirley. Every time you see another hula hoop, remember this moment and how you did something that you thought was impossible. What else could you do that you think is impossible?"

Can Shirley take better care of herself? Can she go back to school? Can she make her new relationship work? \ Can she get out of a bad one? Can she choose to be happier? What choices can she make that will support her dreams? Which ones are we making to support our own?

Choice is your greatest asset because you can choose your thoughts, and your thoughts have magnetic power. They can attract or repel our dreams. Empowered thoughts bring us closer to our desires, and victim-based, "I can't", "I have-to" thoughts push them further away. You can choose to think that anything is possible. You can choose to think that everything is lining up in support of your dreams. You can choose to think that you can change your reaction to any circumstance at any time. You can choose to think that this moment is the only moment you have. You can choose your capabilities. You can choose to design a life instead of accepting one by default. You can choose to see the impossible as possible. You can choose.

Exercise

What are some limiting choices you have made in the past that have kept you small?

_____

_____

_____

_____

What are different choices you can make that will help you grow bigger?

_____

_____

_____

_____

What choices can you make right now to practice new techniques, learn new skills and grow into the Bigger You?

_____

_____

_____

_____

Power Statement

I consciously choose those
thoughts that are in support of
my dreams.

"If you want others to be happy, practice compassion.
If you want to be happy, practice compassion."
— His Holiness the Dalai Lama

The Emotional You

———— ⋈ ————

Compassion Is Your Greatest Strategy

When it comes to dangerous activities, hooping may not be on par with wrestling alligators, but I have physically hurt myself doing it. If I am trying to learn a difficult new move, I can sustain huge purple bruises all over my arms and legs, ripped fingernails, and cut lips. But no hoop injury has compared to the pain I felt upon hearing, "Do we HAVE to see all that?" by a group of fifteen year-old Stepford she-beasts walking by as I was hooping one day. Bam! Flashback to middle school, getting mercilessly made fun of by a pack of deranged sixth-grade girls whose sole mission was to make the fat girl's life a living nightmare. Thanks, ladies. It was delightful being terrified every day by you. Kudos. Physical bruises heal eventually, but obviously, my friend, emotional wounds take time.

Most of us could probably regale each other with stories of schoolyard bullies who called us ugly, fat, skinny, disgusting, stupid, poor or uttered the old standby, "everybody hates you, you know!" Bullies come in all shapes and sizes. They can be on the playground, in the conference room, or in the PTA committee meeting. They are everywhere. They wield their rage in emails, Facebook posts or YouTube comments. They are small people living small lives, so they want everyone around them to feel small too. Emotional wounds hurt, and they are harder to get over. But, once we figure out how to heal our emotional bruises and start choosing better thoughts, we can use the energy that was trapped in our own hurt and redirect it towards the attainment of our dreams. The key to accessing that energy lies in the practice of compassion for oneself and others, joyfully moving from a place of judgment to one of acceptance. When we give more conscious attention to our feelings, we discover that our greatest strategy in the process of creation is COMPASSION.

Practicing Self-Compassion

We are such compassionate beings, yet we are so very, very cruel to ourselves. We don't think twice about sending over a casserole to a sick or grieving friend, helping out a stranger whose car is stuck in a snowbank, and forgiving our children when they make mistakes (even the really BIG ones). Do we treat ourselves in the same fashion? Do we care for ourselves when we are sick? Do we ask for help when we need it? Do we forgive ourselves for not being perfect?

When we can't forgive our bad choices or imperfections, our fear of repeating them will keep us from pursuing our desire for more. Fear is a formidable foe that lurks in our emotional body, ready to trample our desires. We are afraid of being judged. We are afraid of being hurt. We are afraid of being left behind. That fear keeps us small. It doesn't need to keep us small, because all of those things will happen. Whether you like it or not, you *are* being judged by others, you *will* get hurt sometime in your life, and you *will* be left behind someday. If you know these things are going to happen, why be upset when they do? It's simply wasted energy, because this is the gig we all signed up for. So the question isn't how can you avoid those circumstances. Instead, we can ask ourselves the following question: How can we go for our dreams and be good to ourselves, even in the midst of it? When we show ourselves compassion, forgiveness, appreciation, and dare I say, love, we recognize that we don't have to worry about what other people say about us. We don't have to worry about being judged by them.

I always loved the book, *What You Think of Me is None of My Business*, by Terry Cole-Wittaker. Ridding ourselves of judgment is easier said than done, especially since we are so busy doing it ourselves. Have you ever Facebook-stalked an ex, either yours or someone else's? How about obsessively googling your competition? When we are conducting our covert surveillance, we immediately execute a rigorous character assessment. We are either ruthlessly judging our targets or ourselves. "She's prettier than I am. She is smarter than I am. She is skinnier than I am. She's younger than I am. She's more successful than I am." or "She's a boozehound. She's an idiot. She's a floozy. I can tell all of that by the obnoxious way she air-kisses while holding a margarita in the majority of the 217 Facebook photos I scoured." Our organizational espionage and corresponding judge-fest aren't much better. We may use bigger words and headier concepts, but our responses still have judgment all over it. "They have a much more attractive offering. They have a stronger balance sheet. They have a more talented management roster. They have a higher earnings per share." We set ourselves up to feel less-than just by turning on our computers!

Soon after I started hooping, I searched YouTube for "hoopdancing" to see if I could learn a few tricks. That was a mistake. My search results gave me achingly beautiful videos from mesmerizing, gorgeous, perfectly toned goddesses who demonstrated Cirque du Soleil-like hoop craziness like ankle hooping over their heads. To add insult to injury, their costumes consisted of tiny triangles of material held together by strings and beads. Top it off with some adorable furry boots, and I found myself reconsidering my hoop hobby. I am a 40-something Midwestern hoopmom who prefers slow-jam hooping. I couldn't possibly compare myself to HoopGirl, Hoopalicious, Spiral or the hundreds of other impossibly-cool twirling pixies! So, I didn't. Instead, I just tried to be the best hooper I could be, arms flaps and all. I showed myself compassion, giving myself permission to blaze my own trail as a hooper. Hey, maybe I can be the poster girl for the next new style: Granny Hooping!

Act As-if

When I hoop in the dance studio at my local YMCA, I will sometimes slip into a pool of self-judgment. Full-length mirrors have a tendency to elicit that response, especially from someone who spent her life hating her reflection. So as not to bring any of that self-hating juju into my hooping, I take a few moments before I start my practice to get right with myself. I look in the mirror and tell myself that I am amazing. I am beautiful. I am perfect, exactly as I am! You know what? A part of me actually believes it! Every day I try to believe it a little bit more. The more I move in joy, the more I believe it.

Believe in yourself just a little bit more. Accept yourself just a little bit more. It's not enough to just say the words, "I accept myself. I appreciate my gifts. I love myself." You need to feel it. This requires work. An effective way to move into the feeling mode of your own power is to employ the "Act As If" technique. Act as if you already have the life you desire, even if your current landscape looks nothing like it. Try some new power thoughts on for size, see them in your mind's eye, feel them in your bones, and walk around with them for a while. If you want to be a hardcore hooper, act as if you already are one. If you want to be loved by another, act as if you already are wildly adored. If you want to get that promotion, act as if you already have it. If you want to be a little less forlorn today, act as if you already are. Look the part, feel the part, speak the part, think the part, embody the part. Eventually at some unpredictable and indecipherable moment, you will stop acting as if you have the part and you'll just have it. You'll become the person you want to be. It all starts with a feeling.

I have spent more than a decade studying personal empowerment, healing, and spirituality. Even after clocking in hundreds of hours in therapists offices, healing spaces, sweat lodges and sacred circles, I still can turn into a puddle if I read a catty comment from a mean-spirited hater. Some days I am a kick-booty inspirational leader, and other days I am a whiny-baby victim-girl. The goal here is not to be perfect. Rather, the goal is to be compassionate with ourselves when we forget. Start forgiving yourself for not being perfect.

Blinded by the Light

Surround yourself with people, environments and messages that celebrate your gifts. Go into the darker parts of yourself and shine a light on your fears. Don't worry about trying to become Mother Teresa; just be you. But try to be the Bigger You. Be the You that knows your awesomeness. Be the You that doesn't give credence to petty comments from insecure people. Be the You that you are destined to be. Shine your light as brightly as you can. It is not your problem if your light hurts the eyes of those blind to their own power.

When you start joyfully moving from one state to another -- from inertia to activity, from victimhood to power, and from judgment to acceptance -- you will see an effect on those around you. Some will be thrilled that you are reaching your fullest potential, and others will not be so happy. In case you haven't noticed, the world has a fair amount of small-minded, fearful people. They are terrified of what other people are thinking or saying about them, and they are living much differently than they want to be. Your growth will remind them of their poor choices, and they will do anything to take you off your stride. They will plant seeds of doubt. They will suggest you don't have what it takes. They will sabotage. Know that it is out there, and don't judge them too harshly for being driven by their fears. Once we really get the hang of being compassionate with ourselves, we can extend that feeling out to those around us. We can accept, understand and ultimately forgive those poor choices born out of fear. By tapping into our emotions more constructively, we discover that an open heart is the portal through which our dreams to have more, do more and be more start becoming our new reality. You can open doors you never gave yourself permission to step through.

Exercise

What are the deepest, most painful hurts you would like to free yourself from?

_____

_____

_____

_____

Who can you forgive today?

_____

_____

_____

_____

What can you forgive in yourself today?

_____

_____

_____

_____

In what ways can you show more compassion to yourself and others?

_____

_____

_____

_____

Power Statement

I show compassion to myself and
others in all instances.

"I love you when you bow in your mosque, kneel in your temple, pray in your church. For you and I are sons of one religion, and it is the spirit." — **Kahlil Gibran**

The Spiritual You

Spirit Is Your Greatest Ally

Our final stop in the dream machine is the realm of the spiritual. Some may call it God while others may call it Source, the Universe, one's Higher Power, or simply one's inner knowing. If none of those words fit into your belief system, consider it your soul, your Higher Self, or that X factor that makes you, you. Wisdom traditions describe the nature of spirituality as the stillness between the inhale and exhale. It can be difficult to describe, but we all know it when we feel its presence. It's that quiet essence, that Infinite Grace that brings comfort and contentment to our hearts. In this state, we recognize that we are us, but we are also more than us. When we give attention to our metaphysical health and well-being, we discover that our greatest ally in the process of creation is Spirit.

Spirit wants you to have an amazing life! Spirit will be your full-time partner on your journey to have more, do more and be more, if you are humble enough ask for help. Spirit will point you in the right direction when you have lost your way if you are quiet enough to hear the advice. Spirit will give you the strength you need in your darkest hour, if you are grounded enough to accept the support. Spirit will provide a sense of calm and help you realize that everything is unfolding exactly as it needs to, if you are open enough to trust it. Spirit will conduct a Divine orchestration of people, places, events, circumstances, and synchronicity in radical support of your dreams. You don't have to do it all. You don't have to figure it all out. You are not alone.

Sometimes, many times, the challenges we face each day can be so difficult that we get pulled into a downward spiral of depression and powerlessness. Gravity lends its not-so-helping hand by pushing us down, down, down until we crawl to the Barcalounger and into a seemingly safer, sweeter, anesthetized world.

A few years ago, I was in one of those downward spirals. I hadn't yet found joyful movement, and our economic hardship was causing me to live on a steady diet of naughty carbs and Black Box Merlot. I was the biggest I had ever been physically but the smallest I ever was mentally, emotionally and spiritually. Living in a too-big-for-me body and too-small-for-me spirit, every day was physically painful. Every day was depressing. Every day I impatiently waited for the day to end so I could climb back into bed. I preferred living in the cozy confines of dreamland instead of living in the harsh realities of my waking state.

On a cold January morning, Spirit lifted me out of my perpetual funk. Like most people, I made a New Year's resolution to finally lose the weight that had been dogging me for years. Knowing that exercise is just as important as making better food choices, I dusted off my barely-used hoop. Wearing my husband's grey sweatshirt and black sweatpants because they were the only things that fit me, I tentatively gave it a whirl. Due to my sedentary lifestyle, I got winded right away, finding it difficult to continue. My hoop dropped -- a lot. I would muster a few rotations around my Michelin middle, but it would inevitably fall to the ground within a few seconds. I'd pick it up, spin it around, and watch it drop. Over and over and over again. Each time it got harder and harder and harder to pick up off the ground. I grew so angry at myself that I slammed my hand down on the stop button of my boombox and collapsed on the floor in the middle of my hoop. I cried. Hard. You know those kinds of breakdowns where you cry so hard that your throat hurts, your eyes burn and fluids fall freely from your face? Italian grandmother at a funeral hard? It was one of those cries.

Looking back on it, I can't pinpoint a single cause for my outburst. It was a culmination of years of fear, disappointment, and anger that came together in a perfect storm of self-loathing. I cried because my body wouldn't do what I wanted it to do. I cried because I felt like a failure. I cried because I felt so alone. I cried because I was afraid. I cried because I felt so very far away from who I knew I was really was. As I sat sobbing in the middle of the hoop, I grabbed handfuls of belly flesh and yelled, "I hate you! I hate you! I hate you! Why are you still here? Why do I have to live like this? I don't want to be this way any more!!"

As with all meltdowns, fatigue eventually took over and the tears subsided. I had let go and completely surrendered myself to Spirit. I needed help. I needed a roadmap on how to get back into my groove. I needed a sign. Just then, I had a vision of me in the future. I was in a completely different, smaller body. Instead of wearing my husband's sweat clothes, I was in form-fitting black yoga pants and a sassy halter top. I was on stage in front of hundreds of wonderful people sharing a message of joy and power, spinning around with my beautiful hoop doing a graceful, mesmerizing hoopdance. I wasn't a whining ninny; I was HoopWoman. In a flash of insight and intuition, Spirit showed me my potential future while I sat crumpled on the living room floor. It gave me the wisdom, guidance and support I needed to build a better me, a happier me, a bigger me. There's was just one thing I needed to do: Start Now.

I wiped my tears, picked up my hoop, and clicked play. Each time I played with my hoop, I got a little better. The more I played, the more energy I generated. The more energy I generated, the stronger my thoughts became. The stronger my thoughts became, the better I felt. The better I felt, the more I co-created in partnership with Spirit. Little steps become the pathway to transformation if we are willing to get the help we need.

We can ask for and receive all of the healing, guidance, wisdom and peace we need as we travel the rocky roads of life. No matter how hard it gets, we will always have something to lean on. When we step out of the frenetic volley between the regrets of the past and the fears of the future and just be in the moment, we bring a level of sacredness to our experience. In the silence, we recognize that we are more than our bodies, more than our thoughts, and more than our feelings. This unified feeling of presence is what brings us together and binds us to each other. Together, we can joyfully move from an isolated state of aloneness to a connected state of Oneness.

We really aren't all that different from one another. We all have stuff. We all have stories. We all have dramas and traumas. We all have burdens to carry. However, you have the greatest ally available to you 7x24, every day of the year, for the rest of your life. By strengthening your spiritual core, you will have the support you need to unlock your possibilities and turn them into reality.

Exercise

What is your own personal definition for Spirit?

_____
_____
_____
_____

What is your relationship with the Divine?

_____
_____
_____
_____

Are you actively seeking guidance and support from It?

_____
_____
_____
_____

What specific activities make up your spiritual practice, and how often do you perform them?

_____
_____
_____
_____
_____

What are some ways your spiritual practice can help
you to take action immediately and grow big?

_____

_____

_____

_____

Power Statement

I am unconditionally loved,
supported and guided by Spirit
at every moment.

Putting It All Together

———◆H◆———

Now that you know how important the four keys to transformation are and what you can do to utilize them, what are you waiting for? Start now! Click Play on your dream machine! Lead your own joyful movement movement! By remembering that joy is your greatest motivator, choice is your greatest asset, compassion is your greatest strategy and Spirit is your greatest ally, you can and will create that rich, juicy life you desire and deserve. All you gotta do is start... now.

Exercise

It's time to take all that you have learned and put an action plan in place for you to grow big, starting now. What is at least one specific step you will take today to create the life you want?

Action(s) I Will Take to Grow Physically

_____

_____

_____

_____

_____

Action(s) I Will Take to Grow Mentally

_____

_____

_____

_____

_____

Actions(s) I Will Take to Grow Emotionally

_____

_____

_____

_____

_____

Actions(s) I Will Take to Grow Spiritually

_____

_____

_____

_____

_____

How will you continue your growth progress tomorrow and the days after tomorrow?

_____

_____

_____

_____

How will you continue to stay focused on your bigness long after you have set this book down?

_____

_____

_____

_____

What accountability measures can you put in place to maintain your momentum?

_____

_____

_____

_____

Unleash your full magnificence! You are more than you think you are! It's time to create your dreams!

Power Statement

I am ready to embody my fullest
potential and am taking
the necessary steps right now
to grow big.

Resources

————◆·▮·◆————

I would love to continue to support you long after you have finished reading this book. Here are some links of my work that you may find helpful.

TheresaRose.com (Watch my TEDTalk called "The Hoop Revolution"!)

YouTube.com/TheresaRoseTV

Facebook.com/Hoopwoman

Twitter.com/TheresaRose

LinkedIn.com/in/Hoopwoman

The following resources have helped me personally on my journey to bigness, and it is my hope that they will help you too!

Websites

Center for Sacred Studies, http://centerforsacredstudies.org/

Anodea Judith, Ph.D., https://sacredcenters.com/

Deepak Chopra, https://www.deepakchopra.com/

Mary Morrissey, http://marymorrissey.com/

Abraham-Hicks, http://www.abraham-hicks.com/
lawofattractionsource/index.php

Osho, http://www.osho.com

Daily Om, http://dailyom.com/

Marianne Williamson, http://www.marianne.com/

Books

An Angel Called My Name by Jyoti

The Power of Now by Eckhart Tolle

Eastern Body, Western Mind by Anodea Judith

The Seven Habits of Highly Effective People by Stephen Covey

The Alchemist by Paolo Coelho

The Power of Positive Thinking by Dr. Norman Vincent Peale

The Four Agreements by Don Miguel Ruiz

The Happy Hour Effect by Kristen K. Brown

The Greatest Salesman in the World by Og Mandino

You Can Heal Your Life by Louise Hay

Siddhartha by Herman Hesse

Anatomy of the Spirit by Carolyn Myss
The Art of Happiness by His Holiness the Dalai Lama

Movies

The Matrix

Avatar

Gandhi

Lord of the Rings

Kundun

Man on Wire

The Way

Rocky

Whale Rider

Baraka

It's a Wonderful Life

Apollo 13

Working Girl

The Shawshank Redemption

Coal Miner's Daughter

What's Love Got to Do with It

Acknowledgements

I wish to gratefully acknowledge the following people who helped bring *Start Now, Grow Big* into the world, both on the stage and the page: Holly Zelinsky of Nationally Speaking and Angela Cox-Weston of Midwest Speakers Bureau for opening doors for my keynote speaking services, Mark LeBlanc of Small Business Success for his astute business coaching, my spiritual sister and transformational coach Katie Augustine for showing me a bigger frying pan, my friend Kristen Brown for her marketing genius, my sister-in-law Susan Picotte for helping me through my smallness, my incredible assistant Linda Reid for keeping all of the balls in the air, my BFF Jean McManis for always believing in me and helping me to own my awesomeness, and most importantly my amazing daughter Emma and my partner-in-everything, Michael for filling my heart with joy. I love you both more than the Biggest BIG Thing.

Book Theresa

———▸♦◂———

Book Theresa Rose to speak at your next meeting or event!

"Theresa Rose was a motivating and uplifting start to our conference. Attendees loved her sessions, and left energized and excited. Theresa is a bubbly and genuine person who was a pleasure to work with." - Valerie Johnston, Vice President, Education and Special Events, Community Bankers Association of Illinois

Theresa conducts her inspirational performances for organizations who want to help their team members finally take action and move joyfully toward the attainment of their dreams. Depending on your organizational needs, available time and meeting objectives, Theresa can create a program ranging from a forty-five minute keynote to a multiple-day workshop. Her presentations focus on the core issues that keep us small and the practical, effective techniques we can employ to have a more joyful, abundant and productive experience on a daily basis. She helps audiences create more focus, more energy, more courage, and ultimately more power!

For availability and booking information, please call your favorite speakers bureau or contact Theresa directly at 952-456-1670. Visit TheresaRose.com for more information.

About the Author

———•••———

In addition to being a hardcore hoopdancer, Theresa is also a nationally-acclaimed speaker and award-winning author. In 2012, she was absolutely giddy at being named a top five finalist in the "So You Think You Can Speak?" competition at the Annual Convention of the National Speakers Association. That same year, her giddiness was taken to a whole new level when she was chosen to deliver a TEDTalk called "The Hoop Revolution" at TEDxSarasota. She is also incredibly proud to be a member of the prestigious National Speakers Association.

Theresa not only lights up a room when onstage, she also brings some serious mojo to the page. Her first book, *Opening the Kimono: A Woman's Intimate Journey Through Life's Biggest Challenges*, is what Theresa would describe as "a PG-13 Erma Bombeck meets *Sex and the City*." *Opening the Kimono* won not one, but two fancy-pants literary awards, including the Royal Palm Literary Award from the Florida

Writers Association and the Living Now Book Award from Independent Publisher. Theresa's fresh, unorthodox articles on personal empowerment, spirituality and motivation have been published in dozens of magazines and journals. Seen as an expert on personal power, Theresa has been interviewed by CNN.com, NBC, Glamour, Fitness, Good Housekeeping, Women's Day and many other publications. For more information on Theresa, visit **TheresaRose.com**.

www.ingramcontent.com/pod-product-compliance
Lightning Source LLC
LaVergne TN
LVHW021524080426
835509LV00018B/2644